Test your

Management Style

JOHN WILSON

Series editors: GARETH LEWIS & GENE CROZIER

Hodder & Stoughton

the Institute of Management

The Institute of Management (IM) is the leading
organisation for professional management. Its purpose is
to promote the art and science of management in every
sector and at every level, through research, education,
training and development, and representation of
members' views on management issues.

This series is commissioned by IM Enterprises Limited,
a subsidiary of the Institute of Management, providing
commercial services.

**Management House,
Cottingham Road,
Corby,
Northants NN17 1TT
Tel: 01536 204222;
Fax: 01536 201651
Website: http://www.inst-mgt.org.uk**

Registered in England no 3834492
Registered office: 2 Savoy Court, Strand,
London WC2R 0EZ

Orders: please contact Bookpoint Ltd, 39 Milton Park, Abingdon, Oxon OX14
4TD. Telephone: (44) 01235 400414, Fax: (44) 01235 400454. Lines are open from
9.00 – 6.00, Monday to Saturday, with a 24 hour message answering service.
Email address: orders@bookpoint.co.uk

British Library Cataloguing in Publication Data
A catalogue record for this title is available from The British Library

ISBN 0 340 780509

First published 2000
Impression number   10 9 8 7 6 5 4 3 2 1
Year   2004 2003 2002 2001 2000

Typeset by Fakenham Photosetting Limited, Fakenham, Norfolk.
Printed in Great Britain for Hodder & Stoughton Education, a division of
Hodder Headline Plc, 338 Euston Road, London NW1 3BH by Cox & Wyman
Ltd, Reading, Berkshire.

Contents

Introduction

The word style, when used to describe how we do something, can at first appear contradictory. To some it means being in fashion, setting a tone that people will admire. To others it is about being original, unique or even eccentric. The first interpretation suggests a conventional approach, the second is all about individuality and flair, but in practice few people accept this dichotomy and most regard style as a mix of the two. A person with style may well do things that are conventional and widely approved; but the way they do them will have been given an extra something, a personal touch that makes them different and special.

This understanding of the word style, which when applied to management is about combining good practice with personal flair, is what this book is all about.

Ways of testing and improving your management style will be explored as we look at:

- What is management style?
- Leadership
- Leadership style
- Motivation
- Getting results from people
- Delegation
- Communication

What is management style?

Style is a personal quality

Style is a very personal thing and no one describes it better than Sir John Harvey-Jones when in his widely acclaimed book, *Making it happen*, he says, 'Each one of us has to develop our own (management) style, and our own approach, using such skills and personal qualities as we have inherited ... management is an art rather than a science. The artistry lies in the combination of skills, perceptions, intuitions and combined experience which are brought to bear on problems which are continually different and almost invariably unique'.

> *No one can give another person management style; they have to discover and develop it for themselves by detailed and diligent self-analysis and experiment.*

Which style?

There is no ideal style, and great danger in trying to adopt someone else's. Beware also those articles and books extolling you to change your style to one based exclusively on some trendy technique. We are endlessly told to become more *'empowering'*, *'facilitating'*, *'team-oriented'*, *'customer-focussed'* or to use one or other of a thousand different brands of snake oil. The suggestion being that the chosen technique will solve *all* our problems.

This cannot be so. Techniques are important, and managers remain ignorant of them at their peril, but success does not come from techniques alone: *it rests on the much more demanding skill of knowing which technique to use and when.*

Test Yourself

- Are you aware of the most currently available management techniques appropriate to your job?

- Can you be sure you haven't fallen for a 'one technique for all' approach?

Show some personality

Style, we have already agreed, is about doing your job with flair and originality. Finding the right balance between not showing enough flair and being too eccentric is not easy, but there is evidence to suggest that erring on the side of 'being different' is better than a tendency in the opposite direction. Whilst there are some highly successful managers who are quiet and retiring, the vast majority are folk who stand out from the crowd. They are men and women who are not afraid to let their personalities show or to exploit any gifts they have for communicating with, amusing and generally interesting those they meet at every level in society.

Sir Richard Branson, Anita Roddick and Sir John Harvey-Jones may have different personalities, but you could never describe any of them as shrinking violets. They have no fear of being themselves, of saying what they believe to be true or showing confidence in their ability to achieve results. Their actions match what they say; they convince people of their genuineness and good faith; they appear honest and open. Above all they are enthusiastic about what they do; *and about what everyone around them is doing*. They also enjoy their work and make no secret of the pleasure it brings them.

What is the best approach?

All but the most benighted of managers know that you cannot succeed by using the same approach to every situation. Yet many are not aware of the range of possibilities available to them; and those who are are often unsure about when, where and how to use them.

Choosing the best approach to a management problem involves finding your way through a bewildering array of different factors, of which the following checklist is just a short selection of the most obvious ones:

- the situation itself
- your own personality
- the attitudes of the people involved
- recent events
- the urgency and importance of the task
- organisation culture
- long-term strategy
- the cost of failure

Any of these factors, and many more besides, may affect your choice of action. Devising a checklist for each management situation, and testing your chosen approach against each priority factor, is the first, and perhaps the most important, lesson in developing a successful management style.

Is management an art or a science?

From the quotation given earlier, Sir John Harvey-Jones is in no doubt about management being an art or a science –

he believes it is an art. Most current thinking would support Sir John's view, but it was not always so.

For much of the twentieth century there was a belief that management was a science. It was thought that, given the right research, we would eventually discover some grandiose theories and management would then become the straightforward application of proven techniques. Clearly this has not happened, but we must take care not to discredit management science too much. Management techniques are a vital part of the management process; the 'art' is in the skill of applying them in a field where the attitude and behaviour of people are the deciding factors. Cold science must be tempered with intuition and experience when handling situations involving people's feelings and beliefs. Such situations are always different, often far from rational and never without some surprise or another.

Changing times

The shift of emphasis from a 'scientific' to an 'art' approach comes not just from the increased understanding of management in recent years. It reflects also the marked change in attitude to work and social responsibility by people at all levels in society.

The 'them and us' confrontation that has dictated the management styles used in much of industry and commerce since the industrial revolution has finally died and today's least successful managers are those who have failed to come to terms with their bereavement.

The changes of today, if viewed by someone from the 1970s, would appear awesome. Hierarchies have given way to networks and matrices; managers, supervisors and workers are being moulded into teams; entrenched views about demarcation have been replaced by enthusiasm for multi-skilling and employers now offer 'short-term career growth opportunities' rather than jobs for life.

Styles are changing

The obvious effect of these changes on management style has been a shift from an authoritarian to a more co-operative approach to managing people. A workforce has to be led and motivated, not driven and threatened with sanctions. This places emphasis on the so-called 'soft' management skills; what we are beginning to call the emotional competencies. These competencies include leadership, team-building, teamworking, coaching, counselling, interpersonal skills and the ability to persuade and motivate people. Add to this the extra knowledge and communication skills managers will need if they are to apply these competencies, and we find that the intellectual and emotional demands on 'modern managers' are far greater than anything faced by 'bosses' in the past.

? **Test Yourself**

The challenge of managing today is not just the business of acquiring knowledge and competencies; it is about selecting and adapting techniques and then applying them in a style appropriate to the situation. In recent years, have you:

- changed your approach to leadership?

- re-organised your staff into teams?

- increased the time you spend counselling, coaching and mentoring people?

Style continuum

There is a style continuum, a spectrum of approaches extending from 'extremely authoritative' to 'passive acquiescence'. The successful manager is able to find the right point on this spectrum for each situation; moving quickly and smoothly in either direction in order to 'tune' his or her response to the needs of the situation and the reaction of those involved.

There is a danger that managers with more than twenty years' experience will be tempted towards the authoritative end of the spectrum; getting the task completed and making sure people 'toe the line' is what they were trained to do. In contrast, newly qualified managers, affected by the current emphasis on the 'soft skills', may feel they should stay at the other end. Of course both are wrong. There are times when strong management and powerful persuasion are the *only* way to deal with a problem. Equally, there are situations that cannot be resolved except by using a gentle, co-operative style.

Hard and soft are not mutually exclusive styles – both extremes, and all stations in between, have their place and must be used as necessary.

Flexibility and balance

Being able to move quickly and effortlessly across the style continuum is vital, but it is not the complete answer. And if carried out in an obvious and crude manner can even prove counter-productive. Anything that looks like manipulation or some clever trick will soon be spotted by a modern workforce.

Managers must be completely open and freely show their desire to be flexible, fair to all and anxious to keep as many elements as possible in balance. Everyone affected by a management decision should be involved in the decision process whenever possible. In particular, they should be able to feel that they have influenced any debate and that the final conclusion, whilst not pleasing everyone, is at least the result of balanced argument.

Test Yourself

- Are you routinely able to demonstrate this degree of flexibility?

- Do you always try to include those people affected by a decision in the decision making process?

- Are you getting confirmation from your staff to show that you are achieving the right degree of balance and flexibility?

A modern workforce has the right to:

- **Balance** – the conviction that everyone concerned in a management decision has had an appropriate input into the decision making process and that the final outcome, whether they agree with it or not, is the result of balanced argument.
- **Flexibility** – the knowledge that management has taken into account other people's points of view, sought compromise and demonstrated flexibility in

its efforts to satisfy the concerns and interests of everyone involved.

- *Fairness* – there are few grievances that last longer, and cause more damage, than those resulting from an act of unfair treatment. The most devastating events, like redundancies and plant closures, will be better received and the resulting wounds more quickly healed, if their implementation is seen to be fair and equitable. By contrast, a relatively minor change, accompanied by what is seen as the unfair treatment of just a small minority of staff, can have serious consequences and create resentment that lasts for years.

? Test Yourself

Good management is about arriving at a desired business objective while keeping in balance the needs of the various parties affected by the outcome – are you delivering these essential rights to your staff?

Trust

Trust may sound like an old-fashioned word but it represents a timeless concept, and one that has suffered a great deal in the last two decades. The re-organisation, re-engineering, down-sizing and rationalisation programmes of recent times have lost us much of the trust that was once the hallmark of employee relations in our better managed organisations.

Many people feel that the benefits of re-organisation have not always been worth the price of losing this trust and managers now have a heavy responsibility to win it back. Regaining trust by turning back the clock is not an option. It will return only when employers and workers believe that they are once again striving towards the same objective.

Developing staff

For many individuals the greatest change of our times has been the concept of a career. The days when people were trained for working life by one event at the outset of their career is a fading memory for older people and a bizarre fantasy for anyone under thirty. The near inevitability of job mobility and skill redundancy is now widely accepted and people at all levels accept the need constantly to improve and update their skills. The organisation that fails to recognise this, by not providing training and development opportunities for its staff, will soon find that it is losing people and experiencing increasing difficulty when it comes to recruiting replacements.

Whilst the prime responsibility for training and development must be with the organisation and the individuals concerned, managers have an obligation, irrespective of their organisation's policy, to help staff to develop their talents and acquire new skills.

Summary

This chapter has covered a number of basic areas of management style. Before moving on to look at more specific topics it might be helpful to see how your own style measures up.

? **Test Yourself**
Personal style

Personal management style is something unique to each manager and comes largely from the way we use our learned management skills and inherited personal qualities. It cannot be contrived or 'borrowed' from anyone else.

- Are you using your skills and personal qualities to the full and with confidence?
- Are you being honest to yourself – and proud of it?

Management techniques

How well do you keep up to date on new management thinking and techniques? Do you have access to a wide enough range of techniques to meet your needs?

- If you are not happy with your responses to these questions what are you going to do about it?
  - Training?
  - Read more management books and journals?

Art or science?

Management is mainly an art and has become more so in recent years when attitudes to work and relationships between management and workers have changed so dramatically.

- Are you changing with the times?

Enthusiasm

Are you open, honest and enthusiastic in your dealings with people?

Thinking in terms of the scale below, where do you place yourself?

* _____ * _____ * _____ * _____ * _____✓_*

Closed and	Completely
very guarded	open and honest
with people	at all times

Soft/hard approach

We have shown how important it is for a manager to control style across a range from hard to soft depending on the situation and the people involved.

- How confidently can you select the right point on the 'style continuum'?
- How easily can you 'tune' your style to meet variations that develop in complex situations?
- What are you doing to increase the range of your personal 'style continuum' and your ability to work across it appropriately?

Balance, flexibility and fairness

We have tried to show how balance, flexibility and fairness are such important management style qualities.

- *Balance* – Do you seek input from all those affected by a management issue and make sure any decisions are the result of balanced argument? *always time*

- *Flexibility* – Do you show concern for other people's interests and points of view by being as flexible as possible in your choice of actions? *Usually – restraint*

- *Fairness* – Is fairness at the top of your list of considerations when tackling difficult people problems? *Offered cannot*

Trust

- Are you doing everything you can to build and maintain the trust of your staff?
- Is your organisation creating the right climate for trust? If not, are you actively trying to get them to change?

Developing staff

The concept of a career is very different today from what it was only a few years ago and continuous personal development is an essential process for people at all levels.

- Are you directly helping your staff to develop new skills?
- Are you improving your skills as a coach and mentor?

Leadership

Defining leadership

In the endless debate about what makes a good manager, no subject has been more frequently aired than leadership. Management thinkers of all persuasions, from the detached and philosophical to those with more down-to-earth views on the subject, agree that leadership is an essential management skill.

Clearly this leadership thing is important, but what is it? Definitions of leadership are not in short supply. Indeed most people writing about management in the last hundred years have, deliberately or unintentionally, trotted out their personal definition. Sadly these definitions show little consensus or pattern and seem to tell us more about the people writing them than about leadership.

Looking at the views of three well-known writers on leadership and management we get:

Peter Drucker
The only definition of a leader is someone who has followers.

This is a typical Drucker statement – incontrovertible, crystal clear and icily pragmatic.

Sir John Harvey-Jones
Leadership is the art of enabling ordinary people to turn in extraordinary performance.

A perfect reflection of the man himself; warm, enthusiastic about people and rousing.

Hank Boettinger
The essential requirements for a successful leader are:

1. *he must be positive about what he wants to do*
2. *he must be able to explain what he wants to do both to
   potential allies and hostile critics.*

Just what you would expect from the author of *Moving
Mountains* – simple, practical and filled with the confidence
of someone who has made it work.

These three approaches to defining leadership – and there
are many more – serve to prove one point. The way each of
us sees leadership, and attempts to define it, is greatly
affected by our individual personalities and experience.

Attitudes towards leadership have also changed with time.
In the last thirty years, the popular image of a good leader
has moved towards a warmer style and away from that of
the aloof, 'hero' type. At the same time the once sharp
difference between the leader and those being led has been
eroded. This is especially true in industry and commerce
where 'one-among-equals' is the preferred model.

A modern workforce would never tolerate the
superior/subordinate concept of leadership so widely
accepted throughout the first half of the twentieth century.
Individuality is now strongly felt and people resent being
looked upon as some asset or resource. David Price, writing
in the Institute of Personnel and Development journal in
1996, took an elegant swipe at the condescension of those
who still refer to people as assets: '...forget the platitude
"our people are our greatest asset". Assets', he said, 'are
passive entities that organisations control totally. They can
be stripped, frozen or liquefied. Who wants to be an asset?'

Managers versus leaders

The tired old argument about whether organisations need managers or leaders still drags on, fuelling the idea that managers and leaders are two distinct entities. The dichotomy is made worse by so many protagonists claiming that leaders are all we need and dismissing managers as some inferior species. This silly argument has caused many people great confusion and encouraged a flock of management trainers to waste the time of busy managers with their dreary overhead transparencies listing 'bullet points' in support of their claims.

Of course leadership and management are two different things but managing and leading are not mutually exclusive activities. Leadership is not an alternative to management; it is a quality which managers, along with those in many other walks of life, must possess if they are to get things done through people.

Are leaders made or are they born?

Throughout the early part of the twentieth century it was widely believed that leadership was inherited; or if not wholly genetic, then something that could only be acquired by those from a privileged background who had been exposed to the right experience at home and in certain exclusive educational institutions.

Whilst long discredited, this archaic idea still hangs around, convincing perfectly competent people that they lack something a leader needs. The leaders versus managers argument has not helped, since it also suggests that leaders are special people. They are not. Leadership is a personal quality and the form it takes varies enormously with:

- the situation
- the people being led
- the personality of the leader.

There are successful leaders of SAS units, and successful leaders of scientific research teams, but they are different and not necessarily interchangeable. Unfortunately many providers of leadership training appear to ignore this fact and continue to promote a single, rather macho style of leadership.

Charismatic leaders
There are, of course, people for whom leadership comes easily and who are more readily accepted as leaders by those around them. These people (let us call them charismatic leaders) certainly attract followers but they do not always lead them in the right direction. Hitler and many other despots would score highly as charismatic leaders.

Unifying leaders
The leadership required in industry and commerce is one that unifies. We need people who can lead and motivate disparate groups. Charismatic leaders can sometimes be dividers, unifying part of a group but alienating the rest.

> The unifying leader is usually a calm, unobtrusive person who quietly goes about the business of inspiring and uniting people towards a common cause.

How are leaders made?
Action centred leadership
One of the most popular and successful programmes for

leadership training has come from the Industrial Society, an institution that has been pioneering the development of new management ideas since early in the twentieth century.

The Industrial Society is in no doubt that leadership can be learned and their training programmes and publications have helped thousands of managers to improve their ability to lead. At the heart of the Society's approach to leadership is the concept of Action Centred Leadership (ACL). This highly original and seminal concept, devised by John Adair, Britain's most famous leadership expert, promotes the idea that effective leadership is the result of concern for three things: the **task**, the **individual**, and the **team.**

Adair's strikingly simple model, elegantly expressed as three interlacing circles, (see Figure 1) helps people to grasp the central idea of leadership. The idea being that to get results one must take action to:

- achieve the **task**
- build the **team**
- develop **individuals**

Figure 1

Adair summarises the main functions of the three elements as:

Task functions
Defining the task
Making a plan
Allocating work and resources
Controlling quality
Assessing performance against the plan
Adjusting the plan

Group functions
Setting standards
Maintaining discipline
Building team spirit
Motivating and giving the group a sense of purpose
Encouraging communication within the group
Training the group

Individual functions
Dealing with personal problems
Encouraging and motivating individuals
Recognising and rewarding achievement
Using the individual's abilities and talents fully
Training the individual

Gaining the right balance between these three elements is the secret of good leadership. The skillful leader is able to adjust the emphasis given to each element to meet the needs of a given situation or to take advantage of opportunities as they arise.

The Industrial Society's summary of what Action
Centred Leadership involves includes the following
key points:

- Set the task of the team, put it across with enthusiasm
  and remind people of it.
- Set individual targets after consulting; coach each person
  to achieve these targets.
- Delegate decisions to individuals wherever possible and
  when this cannot be done always consult those affected
  before you decide.
- A clear brief is vital. Everyone must understand the plan
  so that teamwork is part of the process from the
  beginning. Brief your team, check for understanding and
  gain commitment to the task.
- To meet objectives, a clear plan is needed. This involves
  gathering information, ideas and suggestions. At this
  point, good leaders will involve and motivate their staff by
  encouraging their ideas and suggestions.
- By involving people, the leader creates an environment
  where individuals work willingly and well. Standing back
  and evaluating is a vital part of this process. However,
  managers should not stand back too far as the team may
  feel it is not being supported. Visible leadership is
  extremely important and this involves 'walking the job' to
  observe, listen and learn.
- Serve people in the team and care for their wellbeing;
  improve working conditions and safety; work alongside
  people; deal with grievances promptly and attend social
  functions.

? ## Test Yourself

Read carefully the seven statements in the above checklist.

- How many of the seven statements would you say are true of your leadership style?
- If your leadership style does not match up to one or more of these statements are you:

  a) able to change easily?
  b) going to need training or some other form of help?

Summary

This chapter has explored what is meant by leadership and established it as a key element in management style.

Types of leaders have been identified, the relationship between leaders and managers clarified and answers given to the question of whether leaders are born or made.

Finally, one of the best known approaches to leadership and leadership training, Action Centred Leadership, has been discussed.

Checklists

The checklists that follow are designed to summarise some of the general points covered in the chapter and also provide an inventory of essential leadership qualities against which readers can compare their own leadership style.

? Characteristics of a good leader

Approachable ☐

Supportive ☐

Readily accepts responsibility ☐

Good communicator ☐

Self-confident (but not arrogant or cocky) ☐

Trusting (and trusted) ☐

Fair (no favourites and no 'black sheep') ☐

Compassionate and thoughtful ☐

Strong sense of direction ☐

Quick to learn from experience ☐

Decisive ☐

Keen to achieve ☐

Objective and analytical ☐

Recognises and rewards the achievements of others ☐

Acceptable to the team (without being 'one of the lads') ☐

Has faith in own judgement ☐

Not afraid of taking risks ☐

Makes things happen ☐

Has vision ☐

? **Good leadership is about:**

Involving people ☐

Solving problems ☐

Setting and agreeing objectives ☐

Planning, monitoring and controlling events ☐

Making good decisions without unnecessary hesitation ☐

Motivating people and gaining their commitment ☐

Recognising and rewarding achievement ☐

Supporting, guiding, training and stimulating individuals ☐

Generating ideas and encouraging others to do so ☐

Inspiring people ☐

Defining roles and responsibilities ☐

Leadership style

Concern for people and concern for the task

The Action Centred Leadership (ACL) approach, discussed in the last chapter, is based on three elements – the task, the team and the individual. Most studies of management and leadership style adopt a two-element approach – people and the task. This is not a radical adjustment since the team and individual elements of ACL are covered by the generality of 'concern for people'.

Testing your leadership style
The variables, *'concern for people'* and *'concern for the task'*, lend themselves to easy and fairly accurate measurement and knowing the relative strength of each provides a useful indicator of leadership style.

The test that follows is designed to give you an indication of how your personal leadership style balances these two variables.

?

LEADERSHIP STYLE QUESTIONNAIRE

INSTRUCTIONS

Listed below are 30 different leadership behaviours.

Respond to each item according to the way you would most likely act as the leader in a working group situation. Although you may not have staff reporting directly to you, in your day-to-day life you have to obtain the co-operation of others, regardless of their status in the organisation.

Circle the appropriate letter to indicate the extent to which you would respond in the described way.

(A) Always
(F) Frequently
(O) Occasionally
(S) Seldom
(N) Never

Test Yourself

1. I would most likely act as the spokesperson of the group .... A F O S N

2. I would encourage overtime work ..... A F O S N

3. I would allow members complete freedom in their work .... A F O S N

4. I would encourage the use of uniform procedures .... A F O S N

5. I would permit the members to use their own judgement in solving problems .... A F O S N

6. I would stress being ahead of competing groups .... A F O S N

7. I would prod members for greater effort .... A F O S N

8. I would try out my ideas in the group .... A F O S N

9. I would let the members do their work the way they think best .... A F O S N

10. I would be working hard for a promotion .... A F O S N

11. I would tolerate postponement and uncertainty .... A F O (S) N

12. I would keep the work moving at a rapid pace .... A (F) O S N

13. I would turn the members loose on a job and let them get on with it .... A (F) O S N

14. I would get swamped by detail .... A F O (S) N

15. I would represent the group at outside meetings .... (A) F O S N

16. I would be reluctant to allow the members any freedom of action .... A F O S (N)

17. I would decide what should be done and how it should be done .... A F (O) S N

18. I would delegate some of my responsibilities and give authority .... A F (O) S N

19. Things would usually turn out as I had predicted .... A (F) O S N

20. I would allow the group a high degree of initiative .... (A) F O S N

21. I would assign group members to particular tasks .... A (F) O S N

22. I would be willing to make changes .... A (F) O S N

23. I would trust the group members to exercise good judgement .... A (F) O S N

24. I would programme the work to be done .... A (F) O S N

25. I would refuse to explain my actions .. A F O S (N)

26. I would persuade others that my
ideas are to their advantage .... A (F) O S N

27. I would permit the group to set its
own pace .... A F (O) S N

28. I would urge the group to beat its
previous record .... A (F) O S N

29. I would act without consulting the
group .... A F O (S) N

30. I would ask that the members follow
standard rules and regulations .... A (F) O S N

asked.

Instructions for scoring

1. Circle question numbers 7, 11, 14, 15, 16, 25, 29 and 30.

2. Give yourself a score in the left hand margin of 1 for
every circled question If you chose S (Seldom) or N
(Never) for that question. *5*

3. Also score 1 in the left hand margin for questions *not
circled* if you chose A (Always) or F (Frequently). *2*

4. Circle your scores for questions 3, 5, 7, 9, 13, 15, 16, 18,
20, 22, 23, 25, 27, 29 and 30.

5. Count your *circled* scores. This is your total for concern
for people. Record the score in the space following the
letter P below.

6. Count the *not circled* scores. This is your total for
concern for task. Record this number in the space
following the letter T.

7. Record the scores for T and P on the graph in Figure 2 and
draw a line for each score to the point where they intersect.

SCORES   T_____   P_____

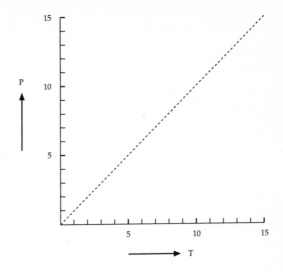

Figure 2

The scores, once plotted on the graph above, illustrate the strength of your concerns for people and for the task. The point where the lines intersect indicates whether you have a tendency towards greater concern for people (your lines intersect above the diagonal) or a tendency towards greater concern for the task (your lines intersect below the diagonal). You should not be unduly concerned if your score shows a significant bias towards either people or the task. There is nothing wrong with such a tendency; most people are firmly on one side or the other. The important thing is to be aware of it and to be prepared to compensate from time to time.

- Do you have a bias to either people or the task?
- Does this information come as a surprise?

A right style of leadership?

Remember, there is no 'right style' of leadership. Right, that is, for every situation. If you are trying to get people to change work practices or re-organise a department, then the approach should be *people centred*; you need to consult and involve people in the decision making process. When there is a plant failure, or a raw material delay, the *task centred* style is more likely to be appropriate.

If the test shows that you have a tendency towards either *concern for people*, or *concern for the task*, do you feel:

- confident you can adjust your style where necessary?
- the need to develop new skills to help you work better in the area to which you do not have a natural tendency?

This need to adjust leadership style to suit the situation is further examined in the remainder of this chapter which explores the way some leading management thinkers have developed the relationship between PEOPLE and TASK.

Blake and Mouton

Dr Robert Blake and Dr Jane Mouton came up with the best-known application of the people/task relationship, the Managerial Grid® (1964, 1978, 1983, 1991: Gulf Publishing, Houston, Texas, and 1999: Grid International, Inc. publications) and a later version (1991, 1999) called the 'Leadership Grid®'. This later Grid is in the form of a two-dimensional model, the variables being measured on a scale ranging from low (1) to high (9).

The Leadership Grid®

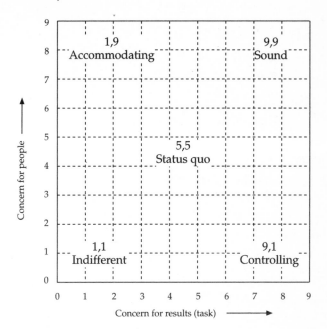

Figure 3

The horizontal axis represents the level of concern for obtaining results, with the term 'results' meaning such things as immediate or long-term goals, productivity or achieving the task.

The vertical axis represents the level of concern for the people involved, including the degree to which a person considers how his or her actions affect others.

Individual Grid styles

The Grid allows us to identify seven distinct styles as

the concern for people and the concern for results interact.

1,1 Indifferent – *Evade and elude*
The key word is neutral. This person goes through the motions of work, doing enough to get by, but rarely attempting to do more.

9,1 Controlling – *Direct and Dominate*
The high concern for results present in this style produces determination, focus and a drive for success. This person is usually well organised, highly trained and has both the confidence to demand high standards and the courage to take calculated risks in order to achieve them. However, a low concern for people limits his or her ability to involve others and the result is a rather forceful approach.

1,9 Accommodating – *Yield and Support*
The high concern for people is a valuable aid to building teams and establishing relationships. This individual maintains a heightened awareness of the feelings, goals and ambitions of others and the effect that his or her actions will have on them. He or she is approachable, friendly and always ready to listen with sympathy and encouragement. However, the low concern for results tends to shift the focus away from task achievement.

5,5 Status Quo – *Balance and Compromise*
The 5,5 person avoids showing particular concern for either people or results and ends up balancing the needs of people and the achievement of results through compromise and trade-offs. The style is characterised by the attitude that 'Good enough or a little better is okay'.

9,9 Sound – *Contribute and Commit*

The 9,9 style is firmly based on logical reasoning and common sense: 'If you have a problem get it out into the open and work through it'. This person is objective and not afraid to tackle difficult issues in an open and honest way. The 9,9 approach gives strength and focus to a team and has the potential for high achievement; but it can run into powerful resistance. Despite being effective, the style can come across as blunt and forceful in organisations where the culture involves playing politics, smoothing over conflict and deferring to authority. Given time, the 9,9 style is usually accepted and its potential for achievement realised.

Paternalistic – *Prescribe and Guide*

The Paternalistic style results from two separate Grid styles coming together. The relationship between the 'paternalist' and the people he or she works with is like that between parent and child where **reward** comes from the 1,9 desire to nurture, and **punishment** comes from the 9,1 desire to dictate behaviour. The result is a person who commands action and achieves results by guidance, praise, reward and subtle punishment.

Opportunistic – *Exploit and Manipulate*

The 'opportunist' approaches every situation with the underlying attitude 'What's in it for me?' and then takes on whatever style is most likely to provide the advantages they seek. Opportunists shift their concerns about as needed to create a convincing facade. They might appear strong and capable of leading in one situation, vulnerable and in need of guidance in another. Everything depends on the situation, the people involved and the potential for personal gain they perceive.

? Test Yourself

Grid styles and self-awareness

The style profiles, described above and set out diagrammatically below, are designed to help you to 'find yourself' on the Grid. Deciding what you would regard as the most suitable behaviour, and comparing this with your actual behaviour, can be a salutary exercise. It also provides a powerful incentive to establish higher standards and develop the skills needed to achieve them.

THE LEADERSHIP GRID®

Where do you fit in?

9,1 Grid Style: CONTROLLING
(Direct and Dominate)

I expect results and take control by clearly stating a course of action. I enforce rules that sustain good results and do not permit deviation.

**1,9 Grid Style:
ACCOMMODATING**
(Yield and Comply)

I support results that establish and reinforce harmony. I generate enthusiasm by focusing on positive and pleasing aspects of work.

5,5 Grid Style: STATUS QUO
(Balance and Compromise)

I endorse results that are popular but caution against taking unnecessary risk. I test my opinions with others involved to assure ongoing acceptability.

1,1 Grid Style: INDIFFERENT
(Evade and elude)

I distance myself from taking active responsibility for results to avoid getting entangled in problems. If forced, I take a passive or supportive position.

9,9 Grid Style: SOUND
(Contribute and Commit)

I initiate team action in a way that invites involvement and commitment. I explore all facts and alternative views to reach a shared understanding of the best solution.

PATERNALISTIC Grid Style
(Prescribe and Guide)

I provide leadership by defining initiatives for myself and others. I offer praise and appreciation for support and discourage challenges to my thinking.

OPPORTUNISTIC Grid Style
(Exploit and Manipulate)

I persuade others to support results that offer me private benefit. If they themselves benefit, that is even better because it helps me gain their further support. I rely on whatever approach is needed to secure advantage.

3-D Managerial effectiveness

Professor Bill Reddin makes a similar model of the relationship between the two orientations by dividing the grid into four squares in which he locates what he identifies as the basic styles of management resulting from different levels of concern for people and the task. He calls these styles – Related, Integrated, Dedicated and Separated (see Figure 4). The *integrated* having a high score for both people and the task; *separated* having a low score for both; *related* having a high score for people and low score for the task; *dedicated* having a high score for the task and a low score for people.

Reddin's four basic styles

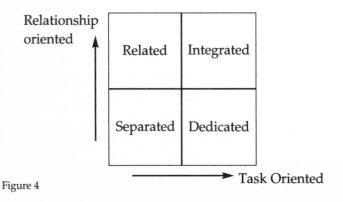

Figure 4

The third dimension
Reddin adds a third dimension – a measurement of efficiency – to construct the 3-D Model shown in Figure 5.

Reddin's 3-D style model

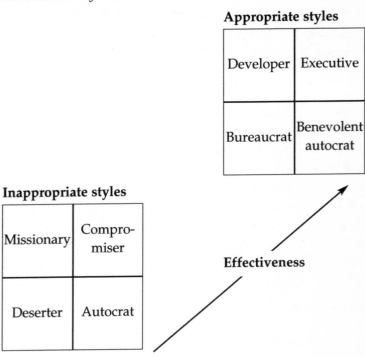

Figure 5

At the lowest level of efficiency, that is to say where the four basic styles are being used in the least appropriate way, he described the role of those occupying the squares as: *Missionary, Compromiser, Autocrat* and *Deserter*.

Moving to the highest level of effectiveness, where the four styles are being used in the most appropriate way, the occupiers of the squares are described as *Developer, Executive, Benevolent Autocrat* and *Bureaucrat*. Reddin's 3-D model, the use of which is described in great detail in his book *How to make your management style more effective*, is helpful for two reasons:

- It illustrates in a powerful way the fact that there is no 'right' management style. Depending on the situation, timing, people involved and many other variables, each of the four basic management styles can be appropriate.
- Reddin's third dimension shows the benefit that comes from using one or other of the styles more *effectively*.

It is the *appropriate* use of the four basic styles that is the secret of Reddin's approach to effective management

In the two boxes below are Professor Reddin's descriptions of the eight management styles that make up his 3-D model (Figure 5). These consist of four appropriate uses and four inappropriate uses of the original basic styles – Related, Integrated, Dedicated and Separated.

Developer – (Related)	Executive – (Integrated)
• Maintains open communication channels • Develops the talent of others • Understands others/supports • Works well with others/co-operates • Trusted by others/listens • When responsible for planning involves many others	• Uses teamwork in decision making • Uses participation appropriately • Induces commitment to objectives • Encourages higher performance • Co-ordinates others in work
Bureaucrat – (Separated)	**Benevolent Autocrat – (Dedicated)**
• Follows orders, rules, procedures • Reliable and dependable • Maintains systems • Watches details/efficient • Rational/logical/self-controlled • Fair/just/equitable • Prefers to write out communications with others	• Decisive/shows initiative • Industrious/energetic • Finisher/committed • Evaluative of quantity, quality and time • Costs, profits and sales conscious • Gets results • Both develops and proposes many new ideas • Shows that efficiency and productivity are valued

Box 1 Four basic styles when used appropriately

Missionary – (Related)	Compromiser – (Integrated)
• Avoids conflict • Pleasant/kind/warm • Seeks acceptance • Makes things easy • Avoids initiating things or giving direction • Unconcerned with outputs or standards • At first sign of conflict, attempts to smooth	• Too much participation • Avoids decisions • Produces grey, acceptable decisions • Idealist • Ambiguous • Sometimes encourages new ideas but does not always follow them up
Deserter – (Separated)	**Autocrat – (Dedicated)**
• Works to rules/minimum output/ gives up easily • Avoids involvement and responsibility • Gives few useful opinions or suggestions • Uncreative and narrow-minded • Hinders others/makes things difficult • Shows little concern about errors and usually does little to correct them	• Critical • Makes decisions • Demands obedience and suppresses conflict • Wants action and results immediately • Downward communication only • Acts without consultation • Feared and disliked • More interested in day-to-day productivity than long-term productivity

Box 2 Four basic styles when used inappropriately

? Test Yourself

Thinking back to some recent management experience:

• Can you identify the style you adopted and see how it fits into Reddin's model?
• Would you, on reflection, use the same style again in a similar future situation?
• Do you feel you were using the appropriate style as effectively as possible?

The Schmidt/Tannenbaum leadership continuum

Authority versus freedom

A different, but equally valid measure of leadership style was devised in the 1950s by W.H. Schmidt and R. Tannenbaum. Their approach was to look at the balance between the extent to which a manager asserts authority and the extent to which the subordinates have freedom to act on their own initiative. The extremes in each case being *total management authority* (implying a very autocratic leadership style) and *complete freedom for the subordinates* (implying abdication by the manager).

The continuum

By accepting there is a range of possibilities between the two extremes, Schmidt and Tannenbaum were able to construct their 'Leadership Continuum' which is illustrated in Figure 6.

The Schmidt/Tannenbaum leadership continuum

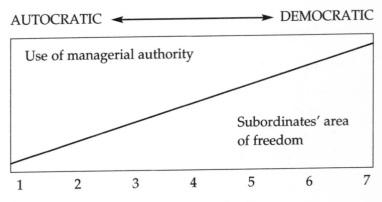

Figure 6

Note that the diagonal line separating the managerial authority from subordinate freedom does not reach the highest and lowest points on the two vertical axes. On the left there is still some subordinate freedom and on the right the manager retains a vestige of control. This reflects a belief that the extremes of autocracy and abdication are never reached. However, managers whose leadership style is to the extreme left of the continuum are acting very autocratically. Conversely, any team whose manager's style is to the extreme right of the continuum is enjoying considerable freedom and a high degree of involvement in decision making.

The seven stages
Schmidt and Tannenbaum divide the horizontal base of the continuum into a 1 to 7 scale and describe a manager's leadership style at each of the seven points as follows:

1. *Tells* – issues instructions.
2. *Persuades* – decides, then explains.
3. *Shows* – presents proposals and invites questions.
4. *Consults* – discusses tentative decisions and is prepared to change.
5. *Asks* – outlines problem and seeks suggestions.
6. *Shares* – defines limits and lets team decide.
7. *Involves* – permits individuals to act within guidelines.

Whilst some unfortunate managers are locked permanently into one or other leadership style, there is no suggestion in this model that a good manager should be restricted in this way. Effective leaders move freely between 1 and 7. Where they end up at any one time will depend on such things as:

- the manager's values and personal management style
- the team's reaction to what is happening
- the team members' attitude towards the manager
- the situation and how this is affected by business, technical and time pressures
- the nature of the problem(s) being addressed.

? ## Test Yourself

Think of some recent instances in which your leadership style was an important factor and see if you can identify the positions you adopted on the continuum.

- Do the positions you adopted seem right with the benefit of hindsight?
- Were you aware of *all* the forces affecting your choice of leadership style?
- With the Schmidt/Tannenbaum model to guide you, would you feel:

  a) more actively in control of your choice of leadership style?
  b) more confident about altering your style as a situation changes and develops?

Summary

Leadership style

In this chapter you have been given the opportunity to test your leadership style and see if you have a tendency towards either concern for people or concern for the task.

Remember your test results are only an indication of your general style. The emphasis you place on people, and on the task, will shift constantly to suit the situation you are in and the problems you are confronting.

Blake and Mouton

The Leadership Grid® provides you with a model against which to compare your own and other people's leadership styles.

Reddin's 3-D model

Reddin's 3-D model, with its extra dimension, provides a more complex matrix in which to locate your personal style and assess how appropriate that style might be for a given situation.

Schmidt/Tannenbaum continuum

The Schmidt/Tannenbaum continuum provides another model against which to test your leadership skill. The continuum is of particular value because it introduces a new and important element in our understanding of leadership; the balance between the degree of *authority* asserted by leaders and the level of *freedom* they give to their subordinates.

The overall objective of the chapter has been to provide you with a variety of ways in which to monitor and improve your performance in that wide range of management activities where leadership style is the dominant factor.

Motivation

There are many occasions in organisational life when good management can improve matters, and bad management can make difficult situations worse, but nowhere are these occasions more frequent than in the area of staff motivation.

The motivating style of some managers is so fundamentally flawed that their sole claim to fame is the ability to knock out of people any motivation they had to start with. Sir Kenneth Corfield, a prominent industrialist in the 1970s, commenting on poor motivation, has said, *'There is no level of poor performance which cannot be reached by groups of people given sufficient discouragement'*.

Motivating a group of people can be a demanding business requiring great skill and patient effort.

De-motivating people is about the easiest task any manager can undertake.

Style is all important

As people's attitude to work is affected more by the way they are handled by managers than by their working conditions, management style plays a key role in motivation. It would seem appropriate, therefore, to take a hard look at the theories and experience-based concepts that help managers develop a 'good motivating style'. We will also try to establish some benchmarks against which you can compare your own management style.

Motivation theories

As motivation is largely about people's attitude to work, it is hardly surprising that psychologists and others concerned with human behaviour have found it an attractive subject for research.

Countless studies and experiments have been carried out since the early stirrings of modern psychology in the late nineteenth century, but employers were at first slow to act on their findings.

Scientific management

Throughout the early years of the twentieth century, the ideas of the so-called 'Scientific Management' movement dominated employers' attitude towards their staff. Pioneers of modern management like Fayol and Taylor rather took for granted the idea that people would work when required to do so and simply gave supervisory management responsibility for making sure they did.

The Scientific Management movement was concerned almost exclusively with production efficiency and in this respect their contribution to the modern world is incalculable. Fundamentally new ideas like the division of labour, production-line manufacturing and inspection-based quality control were all products of the movement; ideas which continue to dominate much of the world's manufacturing industry. However, the movement's views on managing people, and making full use of their knowledge and skill, have now been largely superseded.

The behaviourists

It took until the 1930s for the behaviourists to get an

opportunity to put forward their views and to begin questioning the authoritarian style of the Scientific Management supporters. Credit for the first real breakthrough goes to Elton Mayo, Professor of Industrial Research at the Harvard Business School in the late 1920s and early 1930s.

Mayo's iconoclastic views on motivation were developed when he was famously engaged on experiments at the Hawthorne Works of the American Western Electric Company. These experiments were aimed at finding a way to improve poor productivity.

True to scientific management principles, Mayo set about improving the physical working conditions of an 'experimental group' and comparing its productivity with that of a 'control' group whose working conditions remained unchanged. Things like the lighting were improved for the experimental group and, true to current thinking, productivity improved. However, to everyone's confusion the productivity of the control group also improved; not so much as that of the experimental group but by an amount that was statistically significant.

A second surprise came when the experiment was reversed and the lighting levels were gradually reduced. Instead of going down, productivity continued to increase, even when the lighting was reduced below the levels present at the beginning of the experiment. Only when it was too dark for the workers to see what they were doing did productivity begin to fall.

A number of comparable experiments involving working conditions were carried out and each time produced similar results; productivity increased during the experiments and kept on rising even when conditions were returned to pre-experimental levels and below. Moreover, a smaller but significant productivity increase was noted in the control groups.

Mayo concluded that the increased productivity was not a result of the physical changes he had introduced; it had come about for psychological and social reasons. For the first time in their working lives, these particular workers felt they were being involved in decisions about how they worked. Observers were present throughout the experiments and workers' views and criticisms were listened to and recorded. In short, they were made to believe that management was taking notice of them and that their contribution to the organisation's activities was being recognised.

The Hawthorne Experiments, whilst simple to modern standards, were ground-breaking. They delivered a clear message that people are motivated by more than pay and conditions. The experiments also showed how working in a socially cohesive group could have a positive impact on motivation.

The Hawthorne Effect

The over-riding result of these historical experiments was to show that the motivation of a group of workers could be improved simply by making them feel that management, or some representative of management, was taking an interest in what they were doing. This phenomenon has come to be known as the *Hawthorne Effect*.

Modern motivation theories

Since Elton Mayo opened people's eyes to the importance of the behavioural sciences in motivation, there has been a steady stream of research findings, many of which provide managers with sound, practical ways of motivating staff.

Abraham Maslow
Post second world war, the first of the new wave of motivation thinkers was Abraham Maslow with his famous hierarchy of needs. Maslow suggests that we all have five levels of need and these take effect in a strict hierarchical order. The needs are:

1.	**Self-fulfilment**	realising one's potential; doing what one does best and loves doing.
2.	**Esteem**	having the respect of others; independence; status; pride.
3.	**Social**	being part of a friendly, supportive group.
4.	**Safety**	shelter; security.
5.	**Physiological**	food; air; water.

Maslow points out that we have no choice but to progress from the bottom up through the hierarchy and no desire to move to the next level without first satisfying the needs of the level we are in. Someone who is hungry and thirsty is motivated by nothing but the opportunity to eat and drink. A person who feels insecure and threatened will not be affected by any higher needs until he or she feels safe – and so on up through the hierarchy.

The great lesson we learn from Maslow is that when a working group feels threatened by a lower need (e.g. the security need, when faced with the possibility of losing their jobs) there is no benefit to be gained from offering solutions to higher needs. The motivation process will only begin when the lower, more basic need is satisfied. This explains the crash in morale and motivation that occurs in the workplace at the first hint of plant closure, company sell-offs, redundancy, etc.

Douglas MacGregor
Douglas MacGregor built his theory on an idea that is in direct conflict with the belief that people only work efficiently when closely supervised. MacGregor suggests two approaches to getting results from groups of people.

The first theory, which he call calls 'Theory X', is based on the belief that people have a natural dislike of work and have to be coerced, controlled and directed before they will make any effort. The second theory, 'Theory Y', suggests that work is a natural part of life and people do not have to be forced or threatened in order to work.

However, they do need to be:

- committed to what they are doing
- given recognition for the contribution
- allowed to retain their dignity and self-
- given the maximum freedom possible to
job as they see best.

MacGregor accepts that both theories work, bu. .ne results of 'Theory X' will be low productivity and a de-motivated workforce. 'Theory Y' will produce maximum productivity and a well-motivated workforce.

Needless to say, MacGregor asks us to adopt Theory Y.

Frederick Herzberg

It is widely accepted that the most elegant of the motivation theories is that of Frederick Herzberg. Published in 1959, Herzberg's proposition is the result of a disarmingly simple piece of research. He asked several hundred people about the things that happened to them at work. First he asked what gave them the greatest satisfaction and happiness. He then asked what brought them the greatest dissatisfaction. From the answers to these questions Herzberg concluded that the events and happenings which people reported fell into two distinct and separate groups.

Hygiene factors

The first group Herzberg calls the *'Hygiene factors'*. These are things that create serious motivation problems when not dealt with properly, but once corrected, simply restore the status quo. They do not lead to any extra motivation. These Hygiene factors include:

- organisation's policy and administration
- Supervision and control
- Working conditions, pay and status.

Motivators

The second group, which Herzberg calls the *'Motivators'*, are a series of things that have a positive and lasting effect on motivation.

These Motivators include:

- *Achievement* – most people get considerable pleasure and satisfaction from knowing they have made a useful contribution.
- *Recognition* – it is natural for people to expect and welcome recognition for their achievements and any work they have done well.
- *The job itself* – most us us get our greatest satisfaction from using our intelligence and skill to do our jobs well.
- *Advancement* – the majority of people welcome challenge and want to move on to new things.
- *Responsibility* – only a small number of people are unwilling to accept responsibility; most welcome it, and grow as a result of being given it.

Summary

In this chapter we have tried to show how motivating staff

is a key management skill that requires a knowledge of the behavioural sciences and considerable personal flair.

Motivation is inextricably bound up with leadership and each manager must develop a personal style of leading and motivating. The process of acquiring this style is helped by an understanding of selected items from the mass of behavioural science research that has built up over the last 60 years.

To help find a route into this body of knowledge we began by looking at the seminal work of Mayo and Maslow and then examined the more pragmatic studies of MacGregor and Herzberg.

Whilst there has been much recent research, the ideas of Herzberg still underlie much of what is seen as 'applied motivation science'. A good knowledge of Herzberg's theory will therefore help managers better understand the sometimes confusing attitudes people have to work. It also provides a theoretical base for many of the practical approaches to motivation looked at in the next chapter.

? ## Test Yourself

How does your style match the theories?

Do you:

- recognise the significance of Maslow's hierarchy and accept that basic needs must be addressed quickly and effectively?
- demonstrate a firm belief in MacGregor's 'Theory Y' and protect your staff from any 'Theory X' behaviour coming from other sources?

- accept the difference between Herzberg's 'Hygiene
  Factors' and 'Motivators' and make sure you move
  quickly to do what you can to eliminate problems caused
  by Hygiene Factors:

  - Policy and administration
  - Supervision and control
  - Working conditions, pay and status.

and do you put your maximum effort into achieving for your
staff the Motivators:

  - A sense of achievement
  - Recognition
  - Job satisfaction
  - Advancement
  - Increased responsibility.

Getting results from people
Some practical thoughts on motivation

Whilst the classical theories we have just looked at are helpful in devising a motivation philosophy, they also point to a number of sound, practical ideas for staff motivation. Some of these ideas are explored in this chapter.

Make sure staff know what is expected of them.

> People who do not know what they are supposed to be doing cannot begin to be motivated.

If people are to know what is required of them they must be given definite goals; the more clearly these goals are expressed the greater will be the likelihood of people achieving them.

One way of achieving this clarity is to use the well-established 'four element' format to set goals and objectives. The four elements are:

1. *Measurable* – goals must have both quantitative and qualitative features that are measurable against standards people fully understand and agree on.
2. *Achievable* – tasks must be achievable; asking people to do things that are, for whatever reason, beyond their capability, is very de-motivating.
3. *Challenging* – whilst goals must be achievable, they should also provide some challenge that draws out extra effort. There is little

satisfaction in doing something that is too easy. Tasks that stretch people also develop them.

4. *Time-based* – goals must have deadlines otherwise they risk being set aside. Time targets generate that sense of urgency that most people need to bring out their maximum effort. Time targets should, of course, meet the earlier criteria and be measurable, achievable and challenging.

Write them down

For all but the most simple of tasks, there is a strong case for giving people goals and objectives in writing. The act of writing an instruction helps the writer draw a clear picture of what is being requested. It also helps the person receiving the written instruction to understand what is being asked and makes it less likely they will misinterpret or 'modify' what is being requested.

There is still something to be said for the basic ideas of *Management by Objectives* (MBO), a management technique popular in the 60s and 70s. John Humble, the master architect of MBO, set out the principles of the technique in the imagined words of someone seeking to be well managed (*and well motivated*):

'Agree with me what is expected of me
Give me an opportunity to perform
Let me know how I'm getting on
Help, guide and train me
Reward me according to my contribution.'

Agree the standards required

In most situations it is not enough to know what has to be done and how to do it; people need to know to what standard it has to be done. Not knowing the standard required, and subsequently getting it wrong, can be very de-motivating.

Taking the time to discuss and agree standards as part of the goal-setting process is good management practice. Standards also have to be clear and unambiguous. Remember that the extra time, resources and money needed to do a job that exceeds the required standard can be just as costly as having to repeat work because it falls below standard.

Allocating work

Managers have considerable scope for motivating and de-motivating staff by the way they allocate work. Lack of fairness and obvious favouritism when handing out the 'good jobs' and the 'bad jobs' is perhaps the most common mistake. Showing little or no regard for people's abilities, interests and preferences is another frequent error.

By contrast, the positive benefits of carefully planned work allocation are many and varied. Top of this list is the value to individuals of being given jobs that stretch them and help them develop new skills. We will look at this in more detail in the chapter on delegation.

Listening

Not being encouraged to express their views, or not being listened to when they try to make suggestions, can be frustrating and de-motivating for staff. Finding the time and patience to listen to what people have to say can improve the motivation both of those concerned and that of others who observe the process taking place. *It can also produce some good ideas.*

The authoritarian, macho manager is always a bad listener. Successful management in the twenty-first century involves 'actively' listening to staff and leaving them in no doubt that their views will be noted and properly considered.

Staff must also know that if their ideas are implemented they will receive full credit for any good that results. When people's ideas and suggestions are not practical or appropriate, they should be told exactly why no action is being taken on this occasion, thanked for their efforts and given every encouragement to go on producing more ideas.

Discipline
Discipline should never be about punishment. There are few sanctions available to managers and these should be restricted to serious incidents and applied with a full understanding of employment law. The objective when handling minor disciplinary problems should be simply to change the person's behaviour in the future. *No more is required.*

The secret of a good disciplinary style is *fairness*. Each person must be treated in the same way with no leniency for 'favourites' or harsh treatment for 'black sheep'.

When dealing with discipline matters it is usually helpful to proceed in five stages:

1) Find out why the breach of discipline occurred; what was the cause; is there some reasonable explanation or mitigating factor?

2) Try to get the person to agree that their behaviour was unacceptable.

3) Establish in clear terms where improvement is required and set out the future behaviour that will be acceptable; get the person's agreement to your assessment and their commitment to the planned improvement.

4) Set a time scale for the improvement, if this is appropriate, and in any event make a firm date to review the situation.

5) If, at the review meeting, the person's behaviour has changed as planned then give a word of praise for the achievement and make it clear that the matter is now closed.

Consistent success in dealing with discipline problems is seen by many as a good indicator of general management capability.

Take advice about employment law
Discipline problems vary enormously and this checklist is intended for minor offences. For more serious problems take the advice of a personnel specialist to ensure your actions are within the strict limits of current employment legislation.

Decision making

The way a decision is reached can have a significant effect on how well it is implemented. Effective implementation of a decision is more likely to occur when everyone involved is committed to the idea. Imposed decisions, or those arrived at by a majority vote, are not going to receive as much commitment as decisions resulting from the consensus view of those involved in implementating the decision and those affected by its outcome.

The effort and skill a manger puts into seeking consensus decisions is always well rewarded and success in achieving such decisions is a good measure of management style.

Consensus decisions are always best, but when participation is not possible, for technical, commercial or some other reason, a manager must be prepared to explain the reason behind imposed decisions and justify the effect they may have on the staff involved.

Summary

This chapter has looked at the practical aspects of motivation. In particular it has examined the need to set *goals* and *objectives* that are:

- Measurable
- Achievable
- Challenging
- Time-based

Standards

People need a clear indication of the standards they must achieve. Lack of clarity can lead to work being done either below or above the optimum standard required.

Listening

Listening is not the same as hearing. Listening is a skill requiring effort and concentration. Managers who do not listen to their staff will have problems.

Discipline

Dealing with people who misbehave, fail to carry out their duties or break the rules, is always difficult. Handling discipline situations calls on a wide range of communication, diplomacy, people management and negotiating skills.

Decision making

We have come a long way from the days when managers simply issued orders and workers obeyed. Today the decision-making process has to involve, whenever possible, the people who will have to implement the decisions and those principally affected by them.

? **Test Yourself**

How does your style match these practical suggestions?

Do you:

- let people know what is expected of them?
- discuss with people the standards you would like them to

achieve *and get their agreement that they are achievable*?

- make sure work is allocated fairly and that it presents each individual with tasks that are challenging and rewarding?
- recognise achievement and give praise frequently, convincingly and publicly?
- listen to your staff and take seriously any suggestions they put forward?
- discipline when necessary, but do it promptly, fairly and privately?
- try always to associate reward with achievement, effort and results?
- see that any member of your staff who comes up with a good idea gets full credit from you and from senior management?
- show your staff that you recognise the importance of what they do and appreciate their efforts to do well?
- involve your staff in the decision making process whenever possible and take time and trouble explaining to them *why*, in certain instances, decisions have to be imposed?
- whilst retaining accountability, remove controls wherever possible and encourage staff to accept responsibility for what they do?

Delegation

Why delegate?

A willingness to delegate is common among successful managers and seen by many as the mark of a good leader.

Delegation is not a particularly technical skill; there are no clever techniques that can be learned and applied. In the 'is it an art or a science debate', delegation is definitely on the arts side; it is all about *how* managers go about doing their job, rather than *the job itself*. This makes it decidedly a management style issue.

Those critics of delegation, who say that managers are showing weakness and shirking their responsibilities when they delegate, could not be farther from the truth. Delegating is a sign of strength; it takes courage to give people authority to do things when you have to carry full accountability for the outcome. The safest thing is always to do everything yourself; but the price you pay for not delegating is to be continually busy and unable to stand back from the routine in order to think and plan ahead. For the people who you manage, the price is even higher. For them it means no challenge in their jobs, slow career growth and limited development opportunity.

What is delegation?

There is no confusion about what is meant by delegation in general terms. It is the business of giving someone a task or duty which is normally part of your job.

However, there is some confusion about some of the words we use to describe delegation. One of these words is *responsibility.* We still read in management textbooks that misleading aphorism, 'You can only delegate authority not responsibility'. It is not responsibility that you cannot delegate, it is *accountability.*

To define delegation precisely, we need to be clear about three words. These are:

Responsibility – if you ask someone to do something, and they agree, it would seem a perfectly accurate and modern use of the word to say they had accepted *responsibility* for doing it. In this context, responsibility means a 'contract' to undertake the task or duty.

Authority – this is the key word in defining delegation because it separates real delegation from the simple act of asking someone to do something for you. When we delegate a task, we give a person the *authority* to do it. Authority in this context means the power and right to make decisions and to carry out any actions needed to complete the task or discharge the duty.

Accountability – the thing that cannot be delegated is *accountability.* The person delegating a task must always be held to account for its success or failure.

For all practical purposes the process of delegation can be described using the words *authority* and *accountability* as defined above.

Definition

Managers delegate when they give *authority* to a subordinate to do something which they would normally do themselves and for the outcome of which they remain wholly *accountable*.

For less able managers this precise definition is what makes delegation so hard to accept. It requires them to give up what they would prefer to retain, authority, and retain what they would dearly like to lose, accountability.

Delegation is also about relationships.

However keen a manager might be to delegate, delegation is unlikely to be successful, or even acceptable, if relations with the staff concerned are not good. To delegate effectively there must be complete trust and confidence between the manager and the people to whom he or she is delegating. This trust and confidence cannot be achieved if the manager/staff relations are poor.

The absence of good staff relations is a major obstacle to successful delegation.

What *can* you delegate?

When trying to decide which parts of their job they can delegate, some managers find it helpful to ask themselves the reverse question, 'Which parts of my job should I *not* delegate?' For most people the answer suggests there are few things that should never be delegated. We all have more scope for delegation than we think.

It is less helpful to ask what would happen if you were suddenly forced to be away from work for several months.

In such circumstances your job would usually be done by a mixture of subordinates, peers and senior colleagues who simply have to cope. This is *not* the consciously managed delegation we are talking about and considering such events, real or hypothetical, will not help you to understand the delegation process.

Examining the consequences of a sudden, enforced absence does, however, raise another question: 'What, despite the best efforts of your colleagues, would *not* be done during such an absence?'

The answer to this question can be quite salutary. When measured coldly, in terms of your job description, it usually comes to very little. Looked at in terms of *how* the job is done, the picture can be very different. The 'how you do the job' answer relates not to your 'technical' contribution, which many people can replicate, but to your management style – that unique 'something' you alone bring to the job. This is the bit that others cannot replace; the factor that makes the difference between a manager being simply efficient and being truly effective.

Test Yourself

Take a few minutes to identify the 'how you do it' elements in your management style. Be very honest with your answers: they can tell you a lot.

What *should* you delegate?

It would seem that for most people, and especially confident managers who enjoy good relations with their staff, the number of things that can be delegated is quite large. Clearly you cannot delegate everything, so which tasks and duties should you select for delegation and why?

The simplest and most effective way to select tasks and duties for delegation is to choose those that provide the *maximum benefits*.

Delegation benefits

Delegation benefits separate into three broad categories:

1. *Managers* – Managers benefit by being given the freedom to take on new tasks and spend more time planning, thinking and looking at new ideas and methods.
2. *Staff* – By giving individual members of staff the opportunity to do more challenging and demanding work, they are able to develop new skills, increase their confidence and become more flexible team members.
3. *The organisation* – The organisation benefits from gaining:

   • new ideas, generated by managers released from other tasks
   • fresh thinking from the wider involvement of people in decision making
   • greater efficiency
   • increased productivity
   • a better trained and more flexible workforce.

Where there is a choice of what to delegate, and to whom to delegate, the selection should be based on what best serves one or more of the three categories listed above.

? **Test Yourself**

Is this how you select tasks and duties for delegation?

The decision to delegate

Agreeing to delegate part of your job is an important
management decision and, like all management decisions, it
should only be made after carefully considering the effect
the decision would have on you, your staff, the organisation
and on any products or services to which it relates.

The main things to consider before finally deciding to
delegate fall into three categories:

1. *Quality*
    In most instances you could do the job better and more
    quickly yourself, so you need to balance the 'price' in
    quality and timing against the benefits to you, the
    delegate and the organisation.

2. *Risk*
    There are always risks attached to delegating. These
    include unforeseen problems, unpredictable action by
    delegates and consequential damage when things go
    wrong.

3. *Accountability*
    The manager, as we have already agreed, cannot be
    relieved of accountability for the outcome of a delegated
    task or duty. What this means in practice is that when
    things go wrong, the manager must accept the blame;
    when things go well, the delegate gets the credit.

Before delegating a task or duty, therefore, be sure you
can:

- accept the *risks*

* live with the *consequences* of it going wrong
* be reasonably sure that the *benefits* will outweigh any shortfall in *quality* and/or *timing*.

The process

There are five distinct stages in the delegation process. These are:

1. *Deciding what you want to achieve*
   The delegates must know exactly what is expected of them. This requires you to:

   * give clear, written objectives that are achievable by the delegate (see page 57)
   * make sure the delegates understand the context in which they are working (e.g. their relationship with you and any other people involved); the extent of their authority; the actions they will take when the task or duty is completed.

2. *Selecting the delegate*
   The choice of delegate will depend on several variables. These include the nature of the task or duty; the availability of people; the benefits you would like to derive from the exercise.

   You must ask:

   * who has the appropriate skills (or the ability to acquire them)?
   * who is available (or can be made available by adjusting current workloads)?
   * who would benefit most from the challenge?

- how much help and support will the delegate need (is that help and support available?)?
- what are the risks involved?

3. *Briefing the delegate*

A clear, accurately communicated brief is essential. The briefing process should involve:

- describing the overall task and the context in which it is to be carried out
- talking through the various stages
- checking that the delegate understands fully what is required
- giving the delegate a comprehensive statement of authority and communicating this to *everyone* who needs to know, in particular those who will have to respect that authority if the delegate is to have complete freedom of action
- getting the delegate to prepare a plan and discuss it with you (trying not to force your views on how it should be done)
- establishing the parameters of the task, deadlines, resource limitations and any other factors that might affect the delegate's scope and freedom of action
- making sure the delegate is aware of any sensitive issues
- gently suppressing any excessive enthusiasm and over-confidence
- encouraging and supporting delegates who underestimate their abilities and lack confidence.

4. *Monitoring*

Remember always that it is *delegation* not *abdication*.

Monitoring is essential, but the way this is done should be agreed as part of the plan. To monitor effectively you should:

- establish a programme of periodic reviews and stick to the schedule
- where appropriate, decide on intermediate targets with firm dates for their review
- at the review stages, look out for major errors or misjudgements, but do not worry about small things going wrong
- be available to support and advise, if invited, but do not intervene unless serious problems are about to develop
- encourage delegates to tell you about their mistakes, and the things that go wrong, and discuss these without reprimand or criticism; delegation has a training dimension and things going wrong must be seen as training opportunities rather than setbacks
- progressively stand back from the process and allow delegates to develop their own ways of working once it is clear they have the agreed objectives in mind.

5. *Evaluation*

However important the other reasons for delegating might be, it should always be regarded as a learning experience. The learning value for delegates is, of course, obvious. Less obvious, but often just as valuable, are the lessons that can be learned by you (the manager) and the organisation. To get full value from delegation each event should be carefully evaluated.

The evaluation of a successful delegation will be

different from that of a failed event.

(i)   When the delegation has been successful:
- check that the exercise was carried out according to plan. If it was, this reinforces the planning process. If some things were done differently, these must be separately examined to see what improved methods and new ideas might have been generated.
- talk the delegate through the exercise to make sure he or she has derived the maximum training and development from the experience.

(ii) When the delegation is not successful try to find out exactly why it failed:
- was the wrong person selected?
- were there misunderstandings?
- was the delegate badly briefed?
- was the delegate's performance below normal standards, and if so, why?
- was the task too big for the delegate?
- were there some problems you should have anticipated, but didn't?

The primary objective when evaluating a failed delegation exercise should be to find ways of preventing the same mistakes being made in the future. It should not be a witch hunt. If the delegate was wholly or partly to blame for the failure, take care not to criticise him or her publicly or to senior colleagues.

Summary

Delegation is an important management activity and the

way it is done provides valuable insight into a manager's individual management style. Successful delegation is also seen as a good indicator of leadership skill and people management ability.

Definition

Managers delegate when they give *authority* to a subordinate to do something which they would normally do themselves and for the outcome of which they remain wholly *accountable*.

Staff relations

Delegation is only possible when relations between manager and staff are good. Ironically, delegation, when properly introduced and managed, has the effect of greatly improving manager/staff relations.

What to delegate and to whom

There are several things managers can do to ensure they make the right choice of tasks and duties to delegate and select the best people to serve as delegates.

The delegation process

The delegation process is best managed in a series of five stages:

1. Deciding what you want to achieve from the delegation.
2. Selecting the delegate.
3. Briefing the delegate.
4. Monitoring the delegate

5. Evaluating the completed exercise.

The various checklists that follow are designed to summarise further the delegation process and provide the readers with a model against which to compare their own approach to delegation.

Checklists

? ## Test Yourself

1. The benefits of delegation

This checklist summarises the benefits of delegation. Does your delegating style enable you to get all or most of these benefits?

Benefits for the manager

- Releases time to spend on higher level tasks
- Generates new ideas and new ways of managing the operation
- Improves manager/staff relations.

Benefits to the delegate

- Provides opportunity for growth and development
- Gives a chance to learn new skills
- Broadens experience
- Improves confidence
- Provides challenges that extend the ability to cope with new and more demanding tasks
- Offers opportunity to try out his or her own ideas and techniques.

Benefits to the organisation

- Extends the range of staff skills, producing a multi-skilled and flexible workforce

- Generates new ideas and ways of doing things
- Improves job satisfaction and staff motivation
- Provides practical and effective ways of developing staff
- Complements training programmes by creating opportunities for people to try out learned skills that cannot always be fully exercised in their current jobs
- Improves the quality of career and manpower planning by testing individuals' ability to cope with higher level skills and responsibilities as a prelude to promotion.

2. Barriers to delegation

Throughout this chapter we have noted several barriers to effective delegation but the following checklist provides a more comprehensive summary. This checklist is separated into barriers perceived by the manager and barriers perceived by subordinates. Are you 'guilty' of any in the first list? Have you encountered any of the barriers in the second list?

Managers

- I can do it better myself
- I don't trust other people to do it
- I like doing it
- I want everything done 'properly' – I'm a perfectionist
- I am not prepared to take risks
- It takes too long to explain things
- Why should I give away my secrets
- I find it hard to explain things to people
- What happens to me if they do it better than I can?
- It takes twice as long sorting out the mistakes than doing it myself

Subordinates

- It's not in my job description
- Will I get paid extra?

- I have too much to do already
- I don't want to take on the responsibility
- What happens if I get it wrong?
- I don't know enough about it – I've had no experience
- Why are they asking me? Why not ask Doris – she's not as busy as me?
- If I do it once they'll have me doing it all the time.

3. Common Mistakes

Listed below are some of the commonest mistakes made by managers and subordinates involved in delegation. How does this compare with your experience?

Managers

- Not letting go
- Interfering too much
- Checking progress behind the delegate's back
- Dumping work on people at short notice and with inadequate information and guidance
- Seeing delegation as nothing more than a way to lighten the workload
- Failing to use delegation as a training and development opportunity for subordinates
- Over-estimating delegates' ability
- Not reviewing progress regularly
- Failing to evaluate.

Subordinates

- Over-confident – inclined to rush in without proper planning and preparation
- Under-confident – moving too slowly and cautiously; not convinced of their ability and potential
- Seeing delegation simply as extra work rather than an opportunity for growth and development.

4. Are you under-delegating?

The following checklist is designed to help you assess whether or not you are delegating sufficiently. Many managers do not delegate as much as they could.

- Do you work longer hours than people doing work similar to yours?
- Do you work longer hours than any of your staff?
- Do you spend time on work your staff could do for themselves?
- Are you spending more time on detail work than you do planning and exploring new ideas?
- Are you continually being interrupted by people coming to you for decisions they could easily make themselves were you to authorise them?
- Do you hang on to easily delegated jobs because you like doing them?
- Do you feel you cannot trust your staff with work that is more important or demanding than their basic duties?
- Are you worried that if you delegate too much your job might become redundant?
- Your boss doesn't delegate to you so you are not going to delegate to your people.
- Your job might lose some of its 'magic' and importance if junior staff are seen to be capable of doing parts of it.

Communication

In his book *Using Words*, John Casson skillfully reduces all the complex problems of delivering good communication to just two questions:

- 'How do we put ideas into words that are intelligible and acceptable both to ourselves and others?
- How do we balance what we want to say with consideration for the feelings of others so that our words do not cause anxiety to any of them?'

It is hard to imagine a more comprehensive test of communication skill than that posed by these two simple questions. Any manager who finds satisfactory answers to both questions has mastered the art of effective communication.

Communication style

As well as being a routine management skill, communication provides the only means we have for expressing thoughts and promoting ideas. Because of this we find that communication in the work environment takes place at two levels:

- *routine* communication
- *promotional* communication.

Routine communication is essentially reactive: it reflects the culture of the organisation, follows a set of rules and requires attention to detail and protocol. Promotional communication is proactive: it opens up opportunities for individuals to put forward their personal views and influence other people's thinking.

Again we have an example of the difference between efficiency and effectiveness. The manager who masters routine communication is going to be *efficient*. The manager who is able to go beyond that, and use communication in a proactive way, is going to be *effective*.

How much of your time is spent communicating?

We spend a lot of our working time 'communicating to' and being 'communicated with' and it would make sense to start by looking at how this time is employed.

?

Test Yourself

Communication audit exercise

The following exercise will tell you something about the way you communicate and throw some light on your personal communication style.

Answer the questions as accurately as you can, and be prepared for a surprise when you see how much of your time is taken up with communicating.

You may find that after completing Sections 2 and 3 you have to think again about your answer in Section 1.

Section 1

Estimate the percentage of your total working time that is devoted to communication in *all* its forms.   _____%

Section 2

What percentage of your communication time, as measured in Section 1 above, do you spend communicating with:

Senior managers	_____%
Subordinates	_____%
Peers	_____%
People outside the organisation	_____%

Section 3

How much of your communication time is spent on:

1. Written communication

Writing letters and memos	_____%
Writing reports, papers, etc	_____%

2. Presentation

Talks, training sessions, public speaking engagements	_____%
Presenting ideas, project results, etc to management and outside organisations	_____%

3. Listening

Attending talks, lectures and presentations.	_____%

4. Reading

Letters, memos and reports	_____%
Books, journals and technical literature	_____%

5. Person to person

Casual conversation	_____%
Telephone	_____%
Meetings	_____%
Interviews (with specialist	

advisers, clients, etc.)   _____%
IT (e-mail, Internet)   _____%

Look again at your response to Section 3. The five sub-sections can be grouped into three distinct forms of communication. 1 and 2 are about *producing* and *sending* communications; 3 and 4 are about *receiving* communication; 5 is about *interactive* communication.

The way individuals' time is divided between these three areas can tell us something about their communication style. A lot will depend on the nature of the job, but in general terms extrovert people spend much of their time on interactive communication. When it comes to sending information, those with a quieter disposition will favour written communication, whereas the extrovert will go for presentation methods (if these are available) or continue to use interactive opportunities like meetings, the telephone and face-to-face exchanges.

How do we communicate?

Getting your message across

Before you even start the process of communicating you need to ask the following questions:

- What is the *precise* objective? What do I want to get across? What action do I expect as a result?
- Who is going to receive the communication? What do they know already? What do they now need to know? What is going to be their likely attitude on receiving it?
- What is the best medium for the communication – memo, group meeting, telephone, one-to-one conversation?
- Is the time right? Will the communication be going out at a convenient time for *everyone* who needs to know and react to it? Will everyone receiving the communication

have a chance to come to you for clarification or discussion? Is anyone being given an unfair advantage/ disadvantage by the timing?
- Do you have *all* the information you need?
- What sort of follow-up might you expect? How are you going to prepare for this expected follow-up *before* sending out the communication?

Preparing the communication

- Whatever medium you choose – report, meeting, one-to-one discussion, memo, letter, presentation – nearly all communication starts as a written text of some sort. When the subject is really important, even a telephone call or informal meeting requires preparation. And preparation means *writing*.
- Is the form of the communication simple and free from unnecessary and irrelevant material? The whole idea of communication is to be understood, so keep it simple and to the point.
- Is it accurate and correct in *all* the details?
- Is it clear? Messages do get misunderstood; sometimes with disastrous consequences. Look hard at what you have written and change anything that carries the slightest risk of being misinterpreted.
- If the communication includes an important decision, has that decision been expressed positively? Will the wording leave *any* room for doubt?

Receiving communication

It is easy to forget that receiving is also part of the communication process. Listening and reading are often neglected skills.

Listening

Listening is *not* the same as hearing. Listening is about what we *do* with the things we hear; it is a conscious process that requires effort and skill. Misunderstanding is the prime cause of communication problems, and whilst failure to listen is not the only reason why misunderstandings occur, it is high on the list of major causes.

Listening is an active process

?

Test Yourself

Below is a list of the things that characterise good, active listening. How does your listening add up?

Before a meeting, talk or some other event where your main task is to listen, do you:

- Make a note of the issues and points that are likely to be raised and prepare your views on them?
- List the issues that interest you most and decide what sort of information you hope to acquire? Make a note of all the questions to which you expect answers?

At the event, do you:

- Sit where the speaker can be seen and heard clearly?
- Make notes and summarise?
- Concentrate on what is actually *being said*, as opposed to waiting for what you expect or would like to hear?
- Give the speaker feedback, e.g. smile, nod in agreement or show by your facial expression when something is not clear?
- Ignore distractions and do not let the speaker's appearance, presentational style, choice of language or

general attitude take your attention away from what is being said?

- Where possible give the speaker a summary feedback and get confirmation that you have understood correctly?
- Think ahead so that you can anticipate where the speaker is going and prepare in your mind the questions you expect to have answered; and if they are not answered by the speaker's presentation, raise them with the speaker at the appropriate time?

Reading

Like listening, the ability to understand what we read is another of those things that most of us take for granted. Sadly it is not that straightforward. Simply reading a report or letter is not enough; understanding requires conscious effort. Misunderstanding written communication is one of the most costly of all human errors in organisational life.

People who are determined to understand what they read follow the simple rules set out below.

?

Test Yourself

Are you a good reader?

Do you:

- take your time reading key documents and *never* act on them until you are totally convinced that your interpretation is correct?
- take care *never to assume* you know what the writer means and always re-read and reflect on a passage until you are sure you have grasped its meaning?
- check with the writer when you do not understand important statements; and if immediate clarification is not

possible, delay any action prompted by the communication until you have that clarification?

- never read books, technical journals or reports without a pencil and paper to hand? *Writing notes when reading is the only certain way of accurately recalling facts and ideas. The process of writing notes also helps understanding and critical analysis of the material.*

Written communication

Keep it short and simple

There is a tried and tested rule which applies to most forms of written communication. This is known as the KISS rule. The letters standing for:

Keep it Short and Simple

What this rule means in practice is:

- use short simple words
- write short, uncomplicated sentences
- make only one statement per sentence
- keep paragraphs short and concerned with only one issue
- write short letters, memos and reports.

Letters, e-mails and memos

Apart from the obvious need to write plain, grammatically correct English, all one needs to do in order to write good letters, e-mails and memos is to apply the KISS rule and follow the general points on communication made earlier in this chapter.

Writing reports

Know your reader

The best reports are written by people who have the knack of putting themselves in the position of their reader. To be a successful writer in any field you must have a 'feel' for what your reader wants; and a good idea of how he or she will react to what you are going to say.

Reports are about answering questions

From a reader's point of view most reports have only one function: to answer questions. This suggests that a good way to begin preparing material for a report is to draw up a list of the questions you think your readers will be asking. Many of these questions will relate to special aspects of the report's subject, but there are a number of general questions that crop up on almost every occasion.

These are:

- Why has it been written?
- What is it supposed to achieve?
- What ideas, issues, problems and needs is it addressing?
- What (and who) will benefit?
- How does it affect me, my department, my function?
- What is it saying that is new?
- Why should I agree?
- What is in it for me?

If it is recommending some particular action:

- How much will it cost?
- How long will it take to do?
- What resources are required?
- Who is going to do what?
- Why change what we are doing now?

The effort and time taken to complete a list of questions, and finding answers to them, will be rewarded many times over by the effectiveness of the finished report and the ease with which it will be written.

Report structure
The secret of good report writing is to make the reader's job as easy as possible. The clarity of the writing will help in this respect but the most important, and often the most neglected factor, is structure. A logical, carefully planned structure allows the reader to move easily through the text and to find the things that interest them quickly and effortlessly. The outline structure given below can be easily adapted for a range of different reports.

INTRODUCTION	What the report is about and how it fits in with other related activity.
OBJECTIVE	The objective of the report, the subjects covered and the writer's terms of reference.
BACKGROUND	Any information that puts the purpose of the report into context (why it was requested, by whom, etc.).
THE FINDINGS	The results of any investigation, research and opinion gathering exercises carried out and an analysis of the information and data they produced.

| CONCLUSIONS | The writer's views on what the findings imply and the conclusions drawn from them. |
| RECOMMENDATIONS | The writer's recommendations for action. |

Reports are important
A report that is well written and easy to read reflects well on the writer. More than a few careers have moved forward more quickly because a senior manager was impressed by a report or some other written work.

Genius or hard work?
Well written reports are the product of hard work not genius. Few people produce poor quality reports because they lack basic writing skill; the reason is usually a lack of effort. For those whose writing ability is not adequate for the task, the best advice is to seek help quickly. Not being able to write well has always affected a manager's career, but never more so than in today's fast moving world of e-mail and other forms of information technology where the ability to write quickly and with clarity is essential.

The report writing process
Reports, like the subjects they deal with, vary greatly and there is no standard writing process that can be slavishly followed each time one is needed. There is, however, a series of stages through which the preparation of any report normally goes. This series is set out below.

Stages in writing a report

- Be absolutely clear about the aims and objectives of the report and check your understanding of any brief you have been given.
- Collect together all the available material relevant to the subject matter and carry out any research needed.
- Decide on the structure (see structure advice page 89) and draw up an outline plan.
- Fit your material, in the form of brief notes and headings, into the plan.
- Check the plan to make sure it follows a clear logic.
- Now, *and only now*, do you start writing the first draft.
- Check the completed draft to make sure the logic is still clear and the material runs smoothly – if you are not happy, change it. *It is less painful to make changes when the text is still at the rough stage. Leave it until later and you have the agony of rejecting or re-working passages which you have spent time and effort writing, editing and refining.*
- Keep on editing and refining the report until you are happy with *every* aspect.

? Test Yourself

Is this the process you follow when writing a report?

Clarity

Clarity is achieved by keeping to simple forms of expression and writing good English. Graphs, charts, diagrams and illustrations can help, but if used to excess, they have the opposite effect. Choose visual material with care, and use it *only* to help the reader's understanding of the text.

?   # Test Yourself

Testing clarity

There is a well-established test for the quality and clarity of written text. This test measures what is known as the 'Fog Index'.

To carry out this test you need a piece of finished text close to 100 words long.

1. Count the number of sentences in the chosen text and work out the average number of words in each sentence.

    $$\frac{\text{Total no of words in the text}}{\text{No of sentences in the text}} = \text{No of words in an average sentence} = (A)$$

2. Count the number of words in the text with *more* than two syllables = (B)

3. The Fog Index is calculated by adding A and B then multiplying by 0.4

    Fog Index = (A + B) × 0.4

The lower the Fog Index the clearer the text. A score of 12 or less means you are writing good, clear English. Anything substantially higher than 12 and you need to work at simplifying your writing style.

Presentation

The most important area of spoken communication is presentation. By presentation we mean public speaking, giving talks and training sessions and presenting ideas and information to groups of senior managers. Presentation is now a routine part of nearly every manager's job. Sadly it is also the part most of them like least and often do badly.

Many people find making a formal presentation at a conference, or to a group of senior managers, the most daunting of all communication challenges.

Why do people dislike making presentations?
Apprehension, and the desire not to look foolish, are the reasons most people give when trying to avoid speaking in public. This is ironic because uncontrolled fear is rarely the reason for poor performance. It is the *absence* of fear that is more likely to bring disaster.

We have all met those 'fearless' people who, at the drop of a hat, will get up and speak about almost anything. Some are good, true naturals, but most are people whose apparent lack of fear is no more than arrogance and insensitivity. These are the crashing bores who can ramble on for hours, quite oblivious to the misery and pain shown by those forced to listen to them.

The feeling of fear when making a presentation is quite natural and can be made to work positively. Good presenters are those who use fear to summon up their best qualities. Ask any actor and you will be told that fear is always there. The trick is controlling it; reducing the negative effects and exploiting the benefits that come from the 'buzz' produced.

So how do we control fear?

For most of us fear is controllable once we have the overall situation under control. Controlling the situation is achieved by *preparation*: knowing what you are going to do, how you are going to do it, to whom, when and for how long. Preparation provides answers to all these, and many other questions, and helps keep the speaker in control.

Presentations are important:

> At some point in most people's careers, success or failure may depend on the quality and effectiveness of a presentation.

Having the skill and confidence to speak well provides a person with three invaluable benefits.

These are the ability to:

- influence people and events
- gain support for one's ideas and projects
- get things moving and make progress

The skill in putting over ideas often proves more important than the ideas themselves.

> It is a sad fact of life that a second-rate idea, well presented, often succeeds where a better idea, badly presented, fails

Making a good presentation

Public speaking and presentation skills are not natural gifts that some people have and others do not. We are not born 'good speakers', we have to work at it. No one can give a good presentation without putting real effort into its preparation and delivery. It follows, therefore, that anyone can become a good presenter providing he or she is prepared to put enough effort into it.

A successful presentation will have:

- a good introduction
- a logical structure
- a memorable ending.

An effective presenter will:

- be enthusiastic about the subject
- want to meet the audience's expectations
- look confident (even if not feeling so)
- gain the respect and co-operation of the audience
- remain always in control.

Stages in preparing and making a presentation

The following steps apply in virtually every situation and should be carefully followed when making a presentation.

1. Set clearly defined objectives.
2. Gather material (facts, data, visuals, etc.).
3. Structure the presentation.
4. Select the visual aids and presentation techniques to be used.
5. Prepare speaker's notes.
6. Check out the venue (if possible) and rehearse the presentation there, or in a place that resembles it.

Summary

In this chapter we have taken a broad look at communication, established its importance and shown what a significant amount of management time it consumes.

The general principles of communication have been explained with special attention given to the 'receiving' skills of listening and reading and the many applications of written communications

The remainder of the chapter was devoted to the key management skills of report writing and spoken presentation.

I hope that the material in this chapter, along with all the assessments and practical suggestions from earlier chapters, have equipped you to explore and measure your performance in a number of key management disciplines and to use this information to develop your personal management style.